CONFUSING CREATURE NAMES

KILLER WHALES ARE NOT WHALES!

By Daisy Allyn

Please visit our website, www.garethstevens.com. For a free color catalog of all our high-quality books, call toll free 1-800-542-2595 or fax 1-877-542-2596.

Library of Congress Cataloging-in-Publication Data

Allyn, Daisy.
Killer whales are not whales! / by Daisy Allyn.
p. cm. — (Confusing creature names)
Includes index.
ISBN 978-1-4824-0962-8 (pbk.)
ISBN 978-1-4824-0963-5 (6-pack)
ISBN 978-1-4824-0961-1 (library binding)
1. Killer whale — Juvenile literature. I. Allyn, Daisy. II. Title.
QL737.C432 A45 2015
599.53—d23

Published in 2015 by
Gareth Stevens Publishing
111 East 14th Street, Suite 349
New York, NY 10003

Copyright © 2015 Gareth Stevens Publishing

Designer: Michael J. Flynn
Editor: Greg Roza

Photo credits: Cover, p. 1 Fred Felleman/The Image Bank/Getty Images; p. 5 Mike Price/Shutterstock.com; p. 7 Jean-Pierre REY/Gamma-Rapho/Getty Images; p. 9 Stephen Lew/Shutterstock.com; p. 11 Evgeniya Lazareva/iStock/Thinkstock.com; p. 13 Karina Wallton/Shutterstock.com; p. 15 (killer whale tail) Tatiana Ivkovich/Shutterstock.com; p. 15 (killer whale underwater) Miles Away Photography/Shutterstock.com; p. 17 Doug Perrine/Photolibrary/Getty Images; p. 19 Rebecca Yale/Flickr/Getty Images; p. 21 Irina Silvestrova/Shutterstock.com.

All rights reserved. No part of this book may be reproduced in any form without permission in writing from the publisher, except by a reviewer.

Printed in the United States of America

CPSIA compliance information: Batch #CS15GS: For further information contact Gareth Stevens, New York, New York at 1-800-542-2595.

CONTENTS

The Largest Dolphin. 4
What's a Mammal? 6
Living Up to the Name 8
Where They Live 10
Killer Colors 12
Super Swimmers 14
On the Hunt 16
Family Life 18
Time to Play! 20
Glossary. .22
For More Information. 23
Index 24

Boldface words appear in the glossary.

The Largest Dolphin

Have you ever seen a killer whale at an aquarium? They're huge animals that can leap out of the water and high into the air! However, killer whales aren't whales at all. They're actually the largest dolphins in the sea.

What's a Mammal?

Dolphins and whales may look like fish, but they're mammals. Mammals are warm-blooded, which means their body **temperature** stays the same no matter how hot or cold it is around them. Female mammals give birth to live young and feed the babies milk from their body.

Living Up to the Name

Killer whales are also called orcas. This name comes from the Roman god of death—Orcus. They got this name because they eat a lot of other animals. This includes seals, sea lions, squid, fish, penguins, and other birds. They even hunt and eat whales and other dolphins!

Where They Live

Killer whales live in all but the hottest ocean waters around the world. They prefer to live near coasts and not out to sea. They are commonly found in cold water in the **Arctic** and near Antarctica.

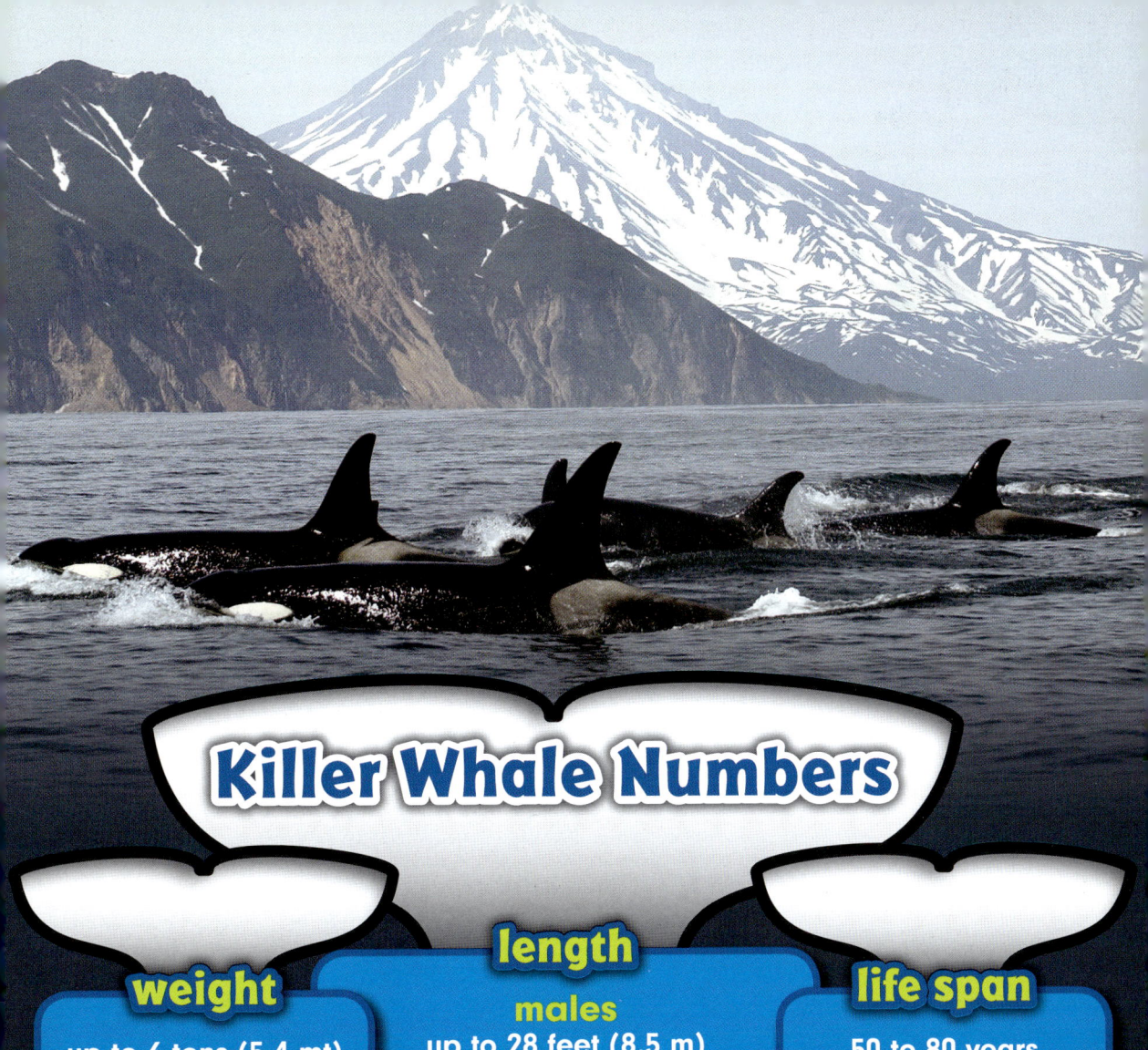

Killer Whale Numbers

weight
up to 6 tons (5.4 mt)

length
males
up to 28 feet (8.5 m)
females
up to 26 feet (7.9 m)

life span
50 to 80 years

Killer Colors

Killer whales are black on top and white on the bottom. This makes them hard to see to fish swimming below them. They also have white **patches** over their eyes and behind their **dorsal** fin.

13

Super Swimmers

Killer whales use their fins and tail to swim quickly. They can dive and stay underwater for about 5 minutes. Unlike fish, killer whales can't breathe underwater. They must come to the water's surface to get air. They breathe through a **blowhole** on the top of their head.

On the Hunt

Like most dolphins, killer whales use clicks and other sounds to find food. The sounds echo, or bounce off of other objects and come back to them. This tells killer whales where the food is and how far away it is.

Family Life

Killer whales live and hunt in groups called pods. These groups often have many family members. Older killer whales may have children and grandchildren in the pod! Adults are very **protective** of young whales, which are called calves.

Time to Play!

Killer whales are very playful animals. They play games with each other and with people. They also like to jump out of the water. If you get the chance to go to an aquarium, you might see an exciting killer whale show!

GLOSSARY

Arctic: the area around the North Pole

blowhole: a body part on the top of the head of a dolphin or other sea mammal that allows it to breathe

dorsal: on or near the back

patch: a small part of something that is different from the area around it

protective: keeping safe

temperature: how hot or cold something is

FOR MORE INFORMATION

BOOKS

Adelman, Beth. *Killer Whales.* Chanhassen, MN: Child's World, 2007.

Claybourne, Anna. *Orcas.* Chicago, IL: Raintree, 2013.

King, Zelda. *Orcas.* New York, NY: PowerKids Press, 2012.

WEBSITES

Killer Whales
seaworld.org/animalinfo/animal-info/animal-infobooks/killer-whale/
Learn much more about killer whales from this SeaWorld website.

Orcas (Killer Whales)
kids.nationalgeographic.com/kids/animals/creaturefeature/orca/
Read more about killer whales and view pictures and videos of them in the wild.

Publisher's note to educators and parents: Our editors have carefully reviewed these websites to ensure that they are suitable for students. Many websites change frequently, however, and we cannot guarantee that a site's future contents will continue to meet our high standards of quality and educational value. Be advised that students should be closely supervised whenever they access the Internet.

INDEX

Antarctica 10
aquarium 4, 20
Arctic 10
blowhole 14
calves 18
coasts 10
colors 12
dive 14
dolphins 4, 6, 8, 16
fins 12, 14
food 8, 16
games 20
mammals 6
orcas 8
pods 18
sounds 16
whales 4, 6, 8

T 576043